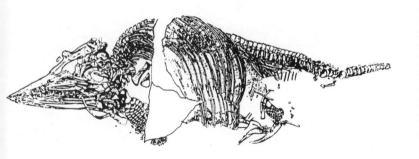

Ichthyosaurus

By Nigel J. Clarke.

FOREWORD

I would like to thank Peter Langham, Dave Costain, Chris Moore and Stewart for their help in writing the book and John Fowles for reading through the manuscript.

The cover drawing is by Tim Montgomery and a poster sized print is available from the Lyme Regis Museum.

1st printed	July 1981
2nd edition	1982
3rd edition	1983
4th edition	1984
New edition	1985

ISBN 0-907683-01-0

Copies of this book can be obtained from:
Nigel J. Clarke, Tollgate Cottages, Tappers Knapp, Uplyme, Lyme Regis, Dorset.

INTRODUCTION

I must presume you would like to see or find some fossils or you would not have bought this book, but I must point out that this book is for the amateur beach rambler, and I do not wish to encourage anyone to climb the cliffs, to do so could be dangerous.

Firstly, if you do not have a map of the local area then a quick orientation is needed. The ideal place to start is at the very end of the Cobb (Harbour) at Lyme Regis. To the east is the town and beyond is Charmouth. Separating these two pretty Dorset towns are the cliffs of Black Ven which rises to 450ft. above sea level. The top is sandy with a sunken plateau area below it. Until 1924 a road, or track, ran along below the cliffs, but in that year it was finally destroyed by earth movement (subsidence).

The Black Ven cliffs are constantly crumbling and falling, and with this action the main fossil-bearing beds continually reveal new material. The debris to the foot of the cliffs is a rich source of varied fossils. With a little patience and rummaging among the fallen rock, you should find the imprints of Ammonities or the 'bullet like' fossil of the Belemnite. In wet weather the flat plateau area above the beach is very boggy as it collects streams of water from the cliffs and becomes dangerous due to the water-logged sands. One should also be very wary of the tide which reaches to the cliffs, towards the Lyme Regis end of the beach.

To the east of Charmouth is the flat-topped cliff of Stonebarrow, 480ft. On the beaches below Stonebarrow and Golden Cap are commonly found washed out pyritized ammonite fossils, these have a distinctive metallic colour. The pyritic ammonites found are small, but because of their unique colouring have been used in jewellery. The cliffs of Stonebarrow slope down to a streamlet known as St. Gabriel's. St. Gabriel's Mouth is the only point between Charmouth and Seatown where it is possible to leave the beach and join the cliff path, though in winter the path up the side of the stream is very slippery.

Golden Cap is to the east of Stonebarrow, and is the most distinguished cliff. It rises to 619ft. above sea level, and is one of the highest points along the south coast. The top is covered with a layer of golden-coloured sand. At the base of Golden Cap are reefs packed with the fossilized remains of belemnites, though these are best seen at low tide.

To the west of the Cobb, Lyme Regis, where the caravans and chalets are, is Monmouth Beach. At the first headland, on the ledges, are the remains of fossilized ammonites, some of which measure over two feet across and are some of the largest species of ammonite known. These remains can only be seen at low tide. The cliffs from the headland due west to Pinhay Bay have a distinct layered appearance. This same outcrop is visible to the east of Lyme Regis. The layered strata are called 'blue lias' and consists of alternate beds of limestone and shale. It is in these beds that large numbers of ammonites are found, and more rarely, crinoids, also most of the area's major fossil finds came from this rock.

In this booklet are sections on the more common fossils that can be found on the beaches of Lyme Regis and Charmouth. I have not gone into detail on the different species of ammonites and belemnites to be found, for information and identification refer to the local (Lyme Regis or Charmouth) library, or I suggest you obtain a copy of the British Museum (Natural History) handbook, British Mesozoic Fossils. I have included the more exotic ichthyosaur and plesiosaur, though the chances of finding an example are very, very remote.

Before you do start fossiling a visit to the Lyme Regis Museum will give you an idea of the type of fossils to be found and in what type of rock. If you do find something out of the ordinary whilst fossiling, then take it to the Museum (Lyme) where you will be put in touch with one of the local experts. It would be as well to place the specimen in a bag, as through bad handling it could be ruined.

Traditionally fossiling is an area of science where the amateur has achieved some notable finds and many of the major discoveries have been achieved by self-taught palaeontologists, and hopefully this will always be so!

Nigel J. Clarke. 1981.

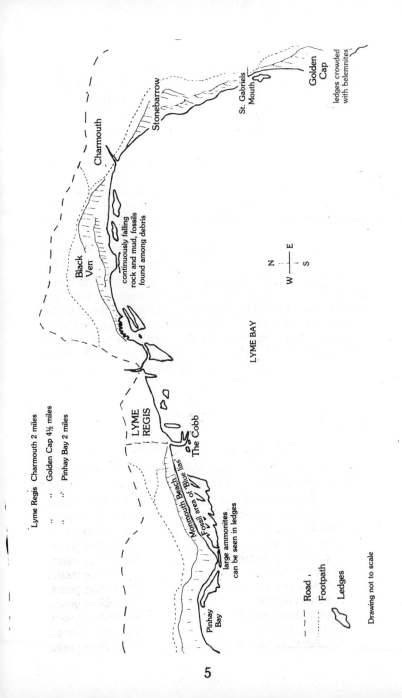

Lyme Regis Charmouth 2 miles

    ,,   Golden Cap 4½ miles

    ,,   Pinhay Bay 2 miles

Charmouth

Black Ven

Stonebarrow

St. Gabriels Mouth

Golden Cap

ledges crowded with belemnites

continuously falling rock and mud, fossils found among debris

LYME BAY

N
W — E
S

LYME REGIS

The Cobb

Monmouth Beach

Fossil area of 'Blue lias'

large ammonites can be seen in ledges

Pinhay Bay

—— —— Road

.... Footpath

⌒ Ledges

Drawing not to scale

THE AGE OF THE EARTH

The Earth is reckoned to be 4,600 million years old, and the fossils to be found around Charmouth and Lyme Regis are only 195 million years old, or younger. To understand the great age of the Earth it can be compared to a year.

January 1st .... Earth formed.
March 15th ... Oldest rocks known found in Minnesota,
U.S.A., 3725 million years old.
November 28th .. First simple plants and animals evolve.
December 1st .... The age of the coal forests.
December 15th .... Heyday of the Dinosaur.
December 31st ..... In the context of this calendar man would not appear on the world until late in the evening.
December 31st ... Three seconds to midnight Columbus discovered the United States.

With regard to the above calendar, the fossils to be found locally would appear from December onwards. (i.e., 195 million years ago). The cliffs were laid down in the Jurassic period. Similar cliffs and fossils are found near Whitby in Yorkshire. In comparison to other rock formation found in Britain the cliffs of Lyme and Charmouth are quite recent in their construction, but are unique in their concentration of fossils.

GEOLOGICAL TIME SCALE

The oldest rocks to be found in Britain are in Scotland from what is called the Precambrian period 570 million years plus.

Cambrian period................ 570 million years.
Ordovician period .... 530 million years.
Silurian period................... 440 million years.
Devonian period .... 410 million years.
Carboniferous period............. 345 million years.
Permian period .... 280 million years.
Triassic period .... 225 million years.
Jurassic period .... 195 million years.
Cretaceous period .... 135 million years.
Tertiary period .... 65 million years.
Quaternary period .... 2 million years.

UPPER CHALK	300ft	
MIDDLE CHALK	100ft	CRETACEOUS
LOWER CHALK	50ft	
UPPER GREESSAND	150ft	
KELLAWAYS CLAY	50ft	UPPER JURASSIC
UPPER CORNBRASH	30ft	
FOREST MARBLE	80ft	
FULLERS EARTH	150ft	
INFERIOR OOLITE	20ft	MIDDLE JURASSIC
BRIDPORT SANDS	200ft	
DOWN CLIFF CLAY	70ft	
JUNCTION BED	3ft	UPPER LIAS
THORNCOMBE SANDS	75ft	
DOWN CLIFF	70ft	MIDDLE LIAS
EYPE CLAY	190ft	
GREEN AMMONITE BEDS	100ft	
BELEMNITE MARLS	80ft	
BLACK VEN MARLS	190ft	LOWER LIAS
BLUE LIAS	100ft	
WHITE LIAS	25ft	
BLACK SHALES	20ft	
KEUPER MARLS	1,300ft	TRIASSIC

7

The rocks in West Dorset are from the Jurassic period and are part of an outcrop that stretches northwards to Yorkshire. The West Dorset rock are lower Jurassic while those to the east are from the upper Jurassic.

How were the Jurrassic Rocks layed down?

During the Jurassic period large parts of present day England was covered by the sea. There were land masses off Brittany (France), Ireland, Cornwall and Wales and a number of Islands such as the Mendips and areas of South Wales. The land masses were low and were drained by great rivers washing down the silt and mud — the resulting rock becoming layered clay and shales. In areas where the water was shallow sands and limestones were formed. The sea around the coast was connected to the oceans and accessible to marine animals. New species evolved and died out, and through the sampling and correlation of fossils found in the rock you are able to tell when the rock was laid down and the approximate age, sometimes a selection of fossils will only be found in a layer of rock 20cm in width. With this method of fossil sampling geologists are able to subdivide the Jurassic rock into further sub-sections.

THE PRINCIPLE STRATA IN THE AREA OF SOUTH WEST DORSET

The White Lias

The white lias can be seen in the cliffs of Pinhay Bay (to the west of Lyme Regis) they are thin bands of white limestone. The fossils found in the rock are small bivalves (oyster) such as Ostrea liassica. The same strata is exposed at the old Quarry workings in Uplyme.

Blue Lias

The word lias is thought to come from the celtic for layered and is a good description of the rock. The layer consists of alternations of clay and lime-stones. There are examples in the cliffs to the east and west of the town. The calcerous matter was originally deposited evenly through the clay though later segregated and formed nodules along the bedding plane, eventually coalascing to form bands of limestone, with their characteristic irregular surface. The blue colour of the rock is due to iron-pyrite.

Fossils from the lower beds include Ostrea Liassic, and Modiola minima and other bivalves. Higher up are the beds of the first zonal ammonites such as Psiloceras planorbis (an ammonite with a smooth shell). Higher exposed layers of limestone contain other ammonites, Coroniceras bucklandi, Lima gigantea, Gryphea arcuata (oysters), there are also areas of Pentacrinus. Rarer, though also found are the bones of Ichthyosaurus and fish bones and scales...

Black Venn Marls

The Black Venn Marls are clay like with bands of fibrous calcite (beef) and as such are referred to as 'shales-with-beef'. Though to the layman this does seem a somewhat ponderous connection. Limestone bands break through the series of shales. The bands contain nodules, some of which are crowded with ammonites.

Fossils found are: Microderoceras birchi which come from above the Shales-with-Beef, Promicroceras planicosta and Asteroceras stellar.

Belemnite Marls

The marl is a lighter grey colour and shows up clearly in comparison to the Black Venn Marls. Belemnites are found in the marl and limestone bands.

Green Ammonite Beds.

The beds are a series of clays containing many species of ammonites though it is the Androgynoceras lanacosta with its chambers filled with green calcite that give the beds their name. Above the bed is nearly 500 ft. of clays with some bands of limestone.

Three Tiers

The Three Tiers can be seen clearly at the base of the Lower Lias between Charmouth and Seatown. The Tiers occur at the start of **Eype Clay** which contains the ammonite Amaltheus margaritatus.

Starfish Bed

Above the Eype Clay is the Starfish Bed named after the numerous brittle star fish that are found. Ophioderma egertoni and Ophioderma tenuibrachiata. Above the Starfish Bed are the **Down Cliff Sands,** and the more distinctive and yellow **Thorncombe Sands** the top of the Middle Lias is shown by the thin band of Marlstone. The **Junction Bed** divides the Middle Lias from the Upper Lias.

The Junction Bed

Dividing the Upper and Middle Lias is a junction bed of limestone which is 3ft thick. The limestone was layed down during a prolonged period of shallowness, such as that which would exist in a lagoon, no clay or sand reached the locality. Ammonites found in this and the Upper Lias include Paltpleuroceras spinatum. The limestone in its history has been subject to long periods of erosion. In Yorkshire the same plane is 300ft thick, while in Dorset a mere 3ft... Above the limestone is the grey **Down Cliff Clay** and the yellow **Bridport Sands**. The latter eventually give way to **Inferior Oolite Limestone**. Once again this plane has been severely erroded and compressed. The remaining layers are of **Fuller's Earth** and **Gault**. Gault fossils may be found in the top area of Black Ven and Stonebarrow. Then comes the layer of **Upper Greensand**, the lowest parts of the Greensands contain hard concretions of sandstone known as cowstones. The last layer of rock is chalk of which little remains, though there are outcrops to the Western cliffs of the town, above Pinhay Bay.

The Lyme Regis 'Volcano'

In 1908 there occurred an event on the cliffs of Black Ven that the local press of the time called the Lyme Regis Volcano. There had been a large fall among the rocks of the Black Ven Marls. The rapid oxidation of the iron pyrites produced sufficient heat to cause combustion among the shales, which were burnt to the appearance of red tiles. The fire was such a good tourist attraction, that when it looked like the flames were to die out the fire was rekindled by a good dousing of paraffin. Similar erruptions have been recorded in Charmouth in 1751, at Golden Cap in 1890 and at Kimmeridge in 1826. At one time some of the Birchi nodules were used as fuel bulkers and were collected from the lowest terrace of Black Ven and from sea level on the mouth of the river Char.

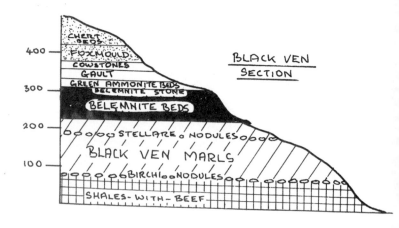

BLACK VEN

SECTION

Church Cliff, Lyme Regis
Showing "Blue Lias".
Stonebarrow in background.

Black Ven
Charmouth foreground

Ammonite
MICRODOCERAS BICHI
Between Charmouth and
Lyme Regis

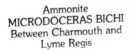

JURASSIC FOSSILS

Weathered remains of an ammonite (on the shore of Monmouth Beach)

Reconstructed Ammonite showing the soft body of the animal.
ASTEROCERAS OBTUSU
(Charmouth)

Ammonite
ASTEROCERAS OBTUSUM

ASTEROCERAS OBTUSUM
Lower Lias
Lower Jurassic (180 M.Y.)
Lyme Regis, Dorset.

ICHTHYOSAURS COMMUNIS
Lower Lias, Lower Jurassic
(180 M.Y.)
Lyme Regis, Dorset.

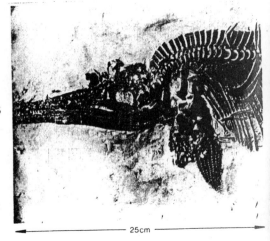

PARKINSONIA PARKINSONI
Upper Inferior Oolite
Parkinsoni Zone
Bajocian (150 M.Y.)
Bridport, Dorset.

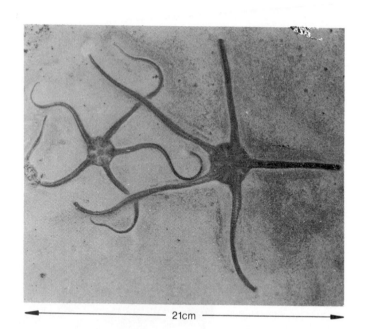

← 21cm →

OPHIODERMA EGERTONI
Middle Lias (160 M.Y.)
Starfish Bed, Bridport, Dorset

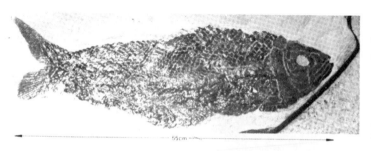

← 55cm →

LEPIDOTES Sp.
Lower Jurassic (180 M.Y.)

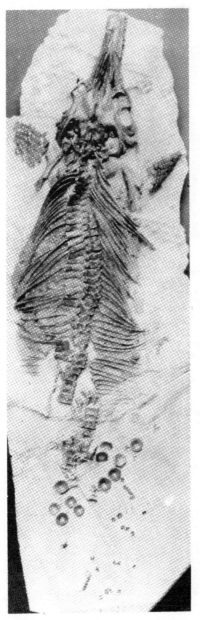

ICHTHYOSAURS COMMUNIS
Lower Lias, Lower Jurassic
(180 M.Y.) Lyme Regis, Dorset.

CORONICERAS Sp
Lower Jurassic
(180 M.Y.)
Lyme Regis, Dorset

15cm

PENTACRINITES FOSSILIS
Lower Lias, Lower Jurassic
(180 M.Y.) Lyme Regis, Dorset.

10cm

Crinoid
PENTACRINITES

BELEMNITES

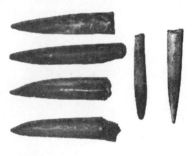

Cut and Polished Ammonite
ASTEROCERAS OBTUSUM

HOPLOPARIA LONGIMANA
(Lobster) Inflatum Zone,
Cretaceous Period,
Charmouth, Dorset.

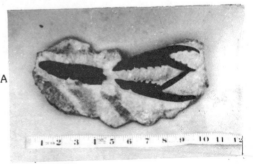

19

ICHTHYOSAUR

Skull of
PLESIOSAURUS

LYME REGIS.

HOW ARE FOSSILS FORMED?

Fossils are the remains of animal or plants preserved in rock. Usually it is only the harder parts of the animal or plant that are preserved, such as the shell, bone or woody fibre. The fossils found in the cliffs and beaches of Lyme Regis and Charmouth are mainly aquatic in origin, which shows that the area was at one time under the sea, the strata in the cliffs having been the sea bed.

The fossils were formed when the carcass or shell of the animal or plant settled on the sea floor, and was quickly covered over by sediment, thus preventing attack by predators or bacteria. As more sediment settles the deposits become layered and compact, various minerals percolating the sediment causing it to cement and form sedimentary rock. A similar system is at work on the organic remains, causing fossilization. The process takes millions of years. Certain minerals give characteristic colouring to the fossils — pyritized fossils have a golden metallic appearance caused by a coating of iron pyrites (fools gold). Unless treated, pyritized fossils do not remain stable, and even when treated they may not remain so.

"Mary Anning"

MARY ANNING

No book about the fossils of Lyme Regis and Charmouth would be complete unless it mentioned some of the biographical story of Mary Anning. Mary Anning was born in 1799 in Lyme Regis, the daughter of a local carpenter, and it was from her father that she learned and gained her passion for fossils. Her father would spend his rest days scouring the cliffs and beaches for fossils, which were sold alongside the fish in her mother's shop. Helped by her father she learned how to spot, extract and clean the fossils.

Mary's father died when she was ten, and she was now expected to earn an income to help support the family. This she achieved by selling the fossils she found locally.

At the age of eleven, in 1811, she made her first discovery of an Ichthyosaurus, the first complete one to be found at Lyme Regis, which was sold to the then Lord of the Manor for £25, and is now in the Natural History Museum in London. It was with this discovery she achieved fame.

In later years her fame was spread by eminent geologists of the time, many of whom visited her. The list of fossils she discovered is impressive and includes the Plesiosaurus and the Pterodactyl.

Illness curtailed her fossiling in later years and she died at the age of 48. Though Mary Anning was never a member of the Geological Society, an obituary and appreciation of her work was read out in the 1848 address. There is a stained glass window dedicated to her memory in the Parish Church at Lyme.

WHAT DO YOU NEED FOR FOSSILING?

The question very much depends on whether or not you wish to collect samples. Many fossils can be found without the need of hammers or chisels, especially the ammonites and belemnites washed out from the rock, which, if you search through the debris on the beach you may be lucky enough to find. Some of the most impressive fossils to be seen are the large ammonites to be found along the beach towards Pinhay Bay, embedded in the ledges.

If you wish to extract fossils from the rocks then you will need the following equipment:—

1. Perhaps the most important is a geological hammer which has both a flat and sharp end. The ordinary house hammer tends to ruin more samples than it recovers.
2. A small chisel.
3. Newspapers and plastic bags to wrap and protect specimens.
4. An old brush.
5. An ordnance survey map of the coast, as it shows how far the tide comes up!
6. A note book, to record where the fossil was found.
7. Protective goggles as often the rock can splinter.

There are also a number of things you should **not** do when fossiling:—

A. **Do not** dig into the base of the cliffs. Apart from being potentially dangerous to you it also causes slips. If you are after samples look in the scree and debris. An ideal place is the rubble outcrops along by Black Venn.
B. **Always know the tides** before setting out, as in many places along the coast the tide comes up to the base of the cliffs. A tide timetable is available from most bookshops in Lyme and Charmouth.
C. **Beware of cliff fall** especially after wet weather.

BELEMNITES (Thunderbolts, Darts)

Resembling a crystalline bullet, the belemnite until the 18th century, was thought to be inorganic, such as part of a stalactite. Normally all that remains is the pointed bullet shaped guard with a cavity in the front, into which the shell fitted. Examples of belemnites have been found where the outline of the soft parts of the body can be seen, and these show a squid-like body.

Belemnites are found in rock all along the Lyme/Charmouth coast and on the ledges off Golden Cap.

Belemnite
reconstructed as it would
have appeared in life.

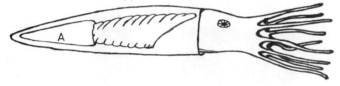

A. Is the hard calcite shell found on the beach.

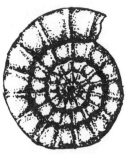 

Echioceras raricostatum
(often found as a pyrited (iron) ammonite)

Promiroceras planicosta.

Asteroceras obtusum. $1\frac{1}{2}'' - 7''$

AMMONITES (Snakestones)

One of the most common fossil found on the Charmouth and Lyme Regis beaches is that of the Ammonite.

An extinct member of the mollusc family, the ammonites lived an estimated 140 million years ago. Their living relatives include nautiluses, squids and cuttlefish. The characteristic shape of an ammonite is a segmented spiral, though the size and segment width varies with different groupings within the ammonite family. Ammonites range in size from 2cm to 1½ metres across.

The name snakestone by which ammonites are also known, originates from Whitby in Yorkshire. Legend describes the infestation of the convent in Whitby by snakes. St. Hilda, then Abbess of the convent, cursed the snakes, decapitating them. The headless serpents then coiled up and died. There was even a prize offered in the 17th century for the finding of a fossilized serpent's head.

A splendid example of an ammonite is built into the wall of Sundial House on Marine Parade (Lyme Regis). Some of the largest ammonites known are embedded in the ledges of Monmouth Beach, towards the headland, examples exceed nearly a metre across. Small pyritized fossils, washed out from the rock, are found on the beaches of Black Venn and Stonebarrow, and have an attractive metal colour.

To see a variety of ammonites found, go to the Lyme Regis Museum, which houses a wide collection of local finds.

Nautilus

The Nautilus pre-dates the Ammonites and has adapted well to its enviroment as species still flourish today. It is the only modern member of this family that still lives in its's shell.

The Nautilus lives on the sea bed feeding on small animals that it catches in its tentacles. The Nautilus only lives in the last section of its shell. The shell is secreted by the animal as it grows, and as the side and lower parts of the body become more active the shell grows in a coiled shape. Each segment is a period of growth which after use is partitioned off and gives the animal bouyancy. The Nautilus can be distinguished from the Ammonite by its less coiled shape and smoother shell.

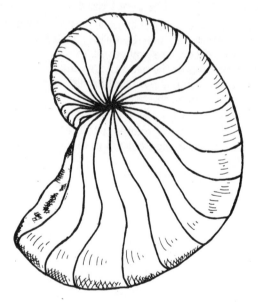

Nautilus

GRYPHEA (Devil's Toenail)

The Gryphea is a fossilized oyster, which has a Gryphea pronounced ridged incurving shell. The fossilized shells are often found in groups cemented to each other, and are common among the Cretaceous sands of Black Venn and Golden Cap. The adult oyster lay on its curved shell, partly embedded in silt, the smaller flat valve open to allow the filtering of food from the water.

Gryphea

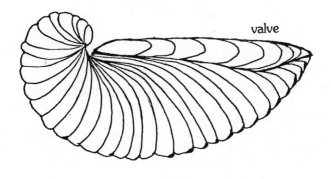

valve

Dapedium.

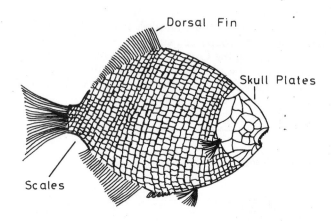

Dorsal Fin

Skull Plates

Scales

FISH FOSSILS

In the Lias clays have been found the fossilized remains of many fish among them the Dapedium. The Dapedium had a lateral shaped body similar to that of a John Dory. The body was covered in thin bony scales with a surface of enamel. The skull also with a covering of bony plates had a small jaw with rounded teeth, used for crushing small crustacea and eating seaweed. The fish, during the Jurassic period were very numerous.

Among the Black Ven Marls are infrequently found the teeth from sharks, though their cartilaginous bodies, which perish, are very rarely found.

TYPES OF FISH FOUND LOCALLY

Acrodus .... Speices of shark, though only the teeth are usually found.

Hybodus.......................... Species of shark.
Eugnathus

Pholidophorus

Dapedium ...... Ganoid fish, small mouth, bony scales.

Shark Tooth

FOSSILIZED VERTEBRA, BONES, TEETH AND COPROLITES

Not everyone finds a complete Icthyosaurus or Plesiosaurus, but on the beaches, where debris has been washed down from the cliff, it is worth looking for the fossilized bones, teeth and vertebrae. Often these fossilized fragments are completely weathered out of the rock, and will only be distinguised from the pebbles and stones by their shape.

Coprolites are fossilized animal droppings, and consist of small bones and other mangled debris. In the Lyme Regis Museum there is a tabletop made from coprolites.

Ichthoysaur Vertebra

Vertebra

ICHTHYOSAUR

Of all the fossils found on the beaches of Lyme Regis and Charmouth the Ichthyosaurus is the most famous. The name ichthyosaur translated from the Latin means "fish lizard", which is a very apt description of the animal. The Ichthyosaur was well adapted to its marine environment. The body of the "fish lizard" was streamlined, similar in shape to that of a porpoise. Propulsion came from the tail, whilst the limbs, structured likes paddles, were for balance and steering. The head is large with a long snout and sharp teeth (though a species has been discovered with no teeth). In the stomach area of the animal the fossilized remains of belemnites and fish scales have been found, illustrating the animal's carnivorous diet.

Complete fossils of the Ichthyosaurus have been found in the blue lias rocks of Monmouth Beach and Church Cliffs (Lyme Regis) though such finds are a rarity. There are several good examples of fossil Ichthyosaurs in the Lyme Regis Museum. The Ichthyosaurus fossil that Mary Anning discovered is now in the British (Natural History) Museum in London, as previously stated.

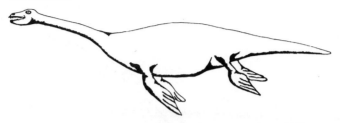

A Plesiosaurus ranged in size from 12 to over 20 ft.

PLESIOSAURUS

Remains and complete Plesiosaur fossils are among the rarer finds. The adult Plesiosaurus was a large, small-headed, long-necked, large bodied reptile. The four limbs were paddle-shaped for its aquatic habitat.

It is the Plesiosaurus that is often claimed to be the 'Loch Ness Monster' though the only ones you are likely to find in Dorset died over a hundred million years ago.

Mary Anning discovered one of the few complete Plesiosaurus skeletons, which after removal from the rock she then sold for the princely sum of £200 to the Duke of Buckingham.

Brittle Star.

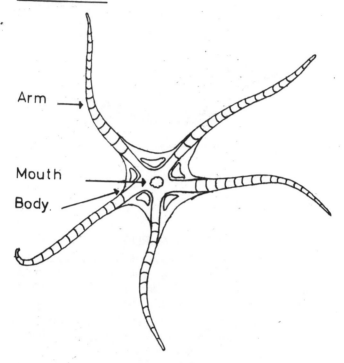

Arm →

Mouth

Body.

·ECHINODERMS

Brittle Stars (Ophioderma egertoni).

Brittle Stars are found in the Middle Lias rock of Stonebarrow and Golden Cap. The animal looks like a thin starfish with five wispy arms. Often, the arms would break off, though re-growth of the missing limb would take place. A brittle-star is also a relative of the crinoid and is rather like a stemless crinoid in appearance, though with the advantage of greater mobility for feeding. The fossil of the brittle-star is often found in groups (beds) though complete examples are rare.

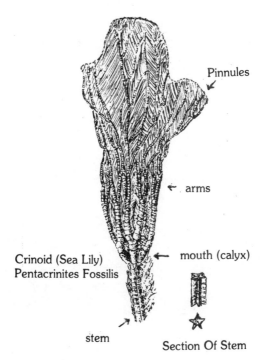

Pinnules

← arms

Crinoid (Sea Lily)
Pentacrinites Fossilis

← mouth (calyx)

stem

Section Of Stem

CRINOIDS. 'Sea Lillies'.

The Pentacrinites in appearance is more akin to a plant than the animal it actually is. The Pentacrinites is a species of 'CRINOID'. The branch like arms would funnel water containing plankton to the mouth located at the junction of the stem.

It is rare to find complete fossil remains of stem, head and arms, but good examples are among the most attractive of fossils to be found. The stem of pentacrinites is star shaped and segmented, broken sections are common. There are two types of crinoid, stem and stemless, that still live in the oceans.

Crinoid fossils can be found on the ledges of Pinhay Bay, which is round and past the headland to the west of the Cobb. In order to reach the ledges you will need to go at low tide.

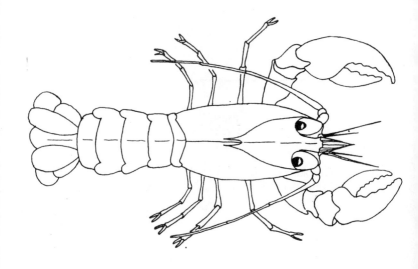

LOBSTER (Latin name: Hoploparia Longimana.)

One of the rarest fossils to be found in the rocks of Lyme Bay is the Lobster. Though smaller then the present day, its body seems to have changed very little. Examples are difficult to extract as the rock is very hard dating from Cretaceous. The measurements of a lobster found by Christopher Moor were 9″ x 3½″ and it was found on the beach to the west of Lyme Regis.